D1094209

BOOKS BY W. S. MERWIN

THE MOVING TARGET   1963
THE DRUNK IN THE FURNACE   1960
GREEN WITH BEASTS   1956
THE DANCING BEARS   1954
A MASK FOR JANUS   1952

Translations

THE SONG OF ROLAND   1963
LAZARILLO DE TORMES   1962
THE SATIRES OF PERSIUS   1960
SPANISH BALLADS   1960
THE POEM OF THE CID   1959

THE MOVING TARGET

W. S. Merwin was born in New York City in 1927 and grew up in Union City, New Jersey, and in Scranton, Pennsylvania. Besides poetry he has written articles, chiefly for *The Nation*, and radio scripts for the BBC.
From 1949 to 1951 he worked as a tutor in France, Portugal and Majorca. Since then he has made the greater part of his living by translating from French, Spanish, Latin and Portuguese. He has lived in England, France and the United States.

THE MOVING TARGET

POEMS BY

W. S. MERWIN

ATHENEUM

NEW YORK

1963

Poems in this collection have appeared in AMERICAN POEMS, A CONTEMPORARY COLLECTION; AMERICAN POETRY NOW; THE BELOIT POETRY JOURNAL; BLUE GRASS; CHELSEA; CONTEMPORARY AMERICAN VERSE; ENCOUNTER; EVERGREEN REVIEW; HARPERS MAGAZINE; THE HUDSON REVIEW; THE LISTENER; THE NATION; THE NEW YORKER; THE PARIS REVIEW; PARTISAN REVIEW; P.E.N. NEW POEMS 1961; POEMS FROM THE FLOATING WORLD VOL. 5; POETRY; POETS' CHOICE; THE SAN FRANCISCO REVIEW; TROBAR

Library of Congress catalog card number 63–20622
Published simultaneously in Canada by McClelland & Stewart Ltd.
Manufactured in the United States of America by
Clarke & Way, New York
Designed by Harry Ford
First Edition

FOR R. P. BLACKMUR

CONTENTS

THE MOVING TARGET

HOME FOR THANKSGIVING

I bring myself back from the streets that open like long
Silent laughs, and the others
Spilled into in the way of rivers breaking up, littered with words,
Crossed by cats and that sort of thing,
From the knowing wires and the aimed windows,
Well this is nice, on the third floor, in back of the bill-board
Which says Now Improved and I know what they mean,
I thread my way in and I sew myself in like money.

Well this is nice with my shoes moored by the bed
And the lights around the bill-board ticking on and off like a beacon,
I have brought myself back like many another crusty
Unbarbered vessel launched with a bottle,
From the bare regions of pure hope where
For a great part of the year it scarcely sets at all,
And from the night skies regularly filled with old movies of my
        fingers,
Weightless as shadows, groping in the sluices,
And from the visions of veins like arteries, and
From the months of plying
Between can and can, vacant as a pint in the morning,
While my sex grew into the only tree, a joyless evergreen,
And the winds played hell with it at night, coming as they did
Over at least one thousand miles of emptiness,
Thumping as though there were nothing but doors, insisting
"Come out," and of course I would have frozen.

Sunday, a fine day, with my ears wiped and my collar buttoned

I went for a jaunt all the way out and back on
A street car and under my hat with the dent settled
In the right place I was thinking maybe—a thought
Which I have noticed many times like a bold rat—
I should have stayed making some of those good women
Happy, for a while at least, Vera with
The eau-de-cologne and the small fat dog named Joy,
Gladys with her earrings, cooking and watery arms, the one
With the limp and the fancy sheets, some of them
Are still there I suppose, oh no,

I bring myself back avoiding in silence
Like a ship in a bottle.
I bring my bottle.
Or there was thin Pearl with the invisible hair nets, the wind
      would not
Have been right for them, they would have had
Their times, rugs, troubles,
They would have wanted curtains, cleanings, answers, they would
      have
Produced families their own and our own, hen friends and
Other considerations, my fingers sifting
The dark would have turned up other
Poverties, I bring myself
Back like a mother cat transferring her only kitten,
Telling myself secrets through my moustache,
They would have wanted to drink ship, sea, and all or
To break the bottle, well this is nice,
Oh misery, misery, misery,
You fit me from head to foot like a good grade suit of longies
Which I have worn for years and never want to take off.
I did the right thing after all.

A LETTER FROM GUSSIE

If our father were alive
The stains would not be defiling
The walls, nor the splintery porch
Be supported mostly by ants,
The garden, gone to the bad,
(Though that was purely Mother's)
Would not have poked through the broken
Window like an arm,
And you would never have dared
Behave toward me in this manner,
Like no gentleman and no brother,
Not even a card at Christmas
Last Christmas, and once again
Where are my dividends?

This is my reward
For remaining with our mother
Who always took your part,
You and your investments
With what she made me give you.
Don't you think I'd have liked
To get away also?
I had the brochures ready
And some nice things that fitted.
After all it isn't as though
You'd ever married. Oh
And the plumbing if I may say so
Would not have just lain down,

And the school children
Would not keep drilling the teeth
Which I no longer have
With their voices, and each time
I go out with a mouthful of clothespins
The pits of the hoodlums would not be
Dug nearer to the back steps.
Maybe you think my patience
Endures forever, maybe
You think I will die. The goat
If you recall I mentioned
I had for a while, died.
And Mother's canary, I
Won't pretend I was sorry.
Maybe you want me to think
You've died yourself, but I have
My information. I've told
Some people of consequence,
So anything can happen.
Don't say I didn't warn you.
I've looked long enough on the bright side,
And now I'm telling you
I won't stir from Mother's chair
Until I get an answer.
Morning noon and night
Can come and go as they please,
And the man from the funeral parlor
To change the calendars,
But I won't go to bed at all
Unless they come and make me,
And they'll have to bend me flat
Before they can put me away.

LEMUEL'S BLESSING

Let Lemuel bless with the wolf, which is a
dog without a master, but the Lord hears his
cries and feeds him in the desert.
CHRISTOPHER SMART: *Jubilate Agno*

You that know the way,
Spirit,
I bless your ears which are like cypruses on a mountain
With their roots in wisdom. Let me approach.
I bless your paws and their twenty nails which tell their own prayer
And are like dice in command of their own combinations.
Let me not be lost.
I bless your eyes for which I know no comparison.
Run with me like the horizon, for without you
I am nothing but a dog lost and hungry,
Ill-natured, untrustworthy, useless.

My bones together bless you like an orchestra of flutes.
Divert the weapons of the settlements and lead their dogs a dance.
Where a dog is shameless and wears servility
In his tail like a banner,
Let me wear the opprobrium of possessed and possessors
As a thick tail properly used
To warm my worst and my best parts. My tail and my laugh bless
    you.
Lead me past the error at the fork of hesitation.
Deliver me

From the ruth of the lair, which clings to me in the morning,
Painful when I move, like a trap;
Even debris has its favorite positions but they are not yours;

From the ruth of kindness, with its licked hands;
I have sniffed baited fingers and followed
Toward necessities which were not my own: it would make me
An habitué of back steps, faithful custodian of fat sheep;

From the ruth of prepared comforts, with its
Habitual dishes sporting my name and its collars and leashes of
    vanity;

From the ruth of approval, with its nets, kennels, and taxidermists;
It would use my guts for its own rackets and instruments, to play
    its own games and music;
Teach me to recognize its platforms, which are constructed like
    scaffolds;

From the ruth of known paths, which would use my feet, tail, and
    ears as curios,
My head as a nest for tame ants,
My fate as a warning.

I have hidden at wrong times for wrong reasons.
I have been brought to bay. More than once.
Another time, if I need it,
Create a little wind like a cold finger between my shoulders, then
Let my nails pour out a torrent of aces like grain from a threshing
    machine;
Let fatigue, weather, habitation, the old bones, finally,
Be nothing to me,
Let all lights but yours be nothing to me.
Let the memory of tongues not unnerve me so that I stumble or
    quake.

But lead me at times beside the still waters;
There when I crouch to drink let me catch a glimpse of your image
Before it is obscured with my own.

Preserve my eyes, which are irreplaceable.
Preserve my heart, veins, bones,
Against the slow death building in them like hornets until the place
    is entirely theirs.
Preserve my tongue and I will bless you again and again.

Let my ignorance and my failings
Remain far behind me like tracks made in a wet season,
At the end of which I have vanished,
So that those who track me for their own twisted ends
May be rewarded only with ignorance and failings.
But let me leave my cry stretched out behind me like a road
On which I have followed you.
And sustain me for my time in the desert
On what is essential to me.

BY DAY AND BY NIGHT

Shadow, index of the sun,
Who knows him as you know him,
Who have never turned to look at him since the beginning?

In the court of his brilliance
You set up his absence like a camp.
And his fire only confirms you. And his death is your freedom.

IN THE GORGE

Lord of the bow,
Our jagged hands
Like the ends of a broken bridge
Grope for each other in silence
Over the loose water.
Have you left us nothing but your blindness?

SEPARATION

Your absence has gone through me
Like thread through a needle.
Everything I do is stitched with its color.

THE DEFEATED

Beyond surprise, my ribs start up from the ground.
After I had sunk, the waters went down.
The horizon I was making for runs through my eyes.
It has woven its simple nest among my bones.

NOAH'S RAVEN

Why should I have returned?
My knowledge would not fit into theirs.
I found untouched the desert of the unknown,
Big enough for my feet. It is my home.
It is always beyond them. The future
Splits the present with the echo of my voice.
Hoarse with fulfilment, I never made promises.

AS BY WATER

Oh
Together
Embracing departure
We hoisted our love like a sail

And like a sail and its reflection
However
We move and wherever
We shall be divided as by water
Forever forever
Though
Both sails shudder as they go
And both prows lengthen the same sorrow

Till the other elements
Extend between us also.

THINGS

Possessor
At the approach of winter we are there.
Better than friends, in your sorrows we take no pleasure,
We have none of our own and no memory but yours.
We are the anchor of your future.
Patient as a border of beggars, each hand holding out its whole
    treasure,

We will be all the points on your compass.
We will give you interest on yourself as you deposit yourself with
    us.
Be a gentleman: you acquired us when you needed us,
We do what we can to please, we have some beauty, we are
    helpless,
Depend on us.

SAVONAROLA

Unable to endure my world and calling the failure God, I will
destroy yours.

INSCRIPTION FOR A BURNED BRIDGE

Not your defeats, no.
I have gone in with the river.
I will serve you no longer but you may follow me.

ECONOMY

No need to break the mirror.
Here is the face shattered,
Good for seven years of sorrow.

13

LOST MONTH

The light of the eyes in the house of the crow. Here the gods' voices break and some will never sing again, but some come closer and whisper. Never their names.

There are no hinges. One side of a door is simply forgotten in the other.

In the windows the permissions appear, already lit, unasked, but the wind is the wind of parsimony, and the shadows, which are numerous and large, strain at their slender leashes. One fine day the first knives come through the mirrors, like fins of sharks. The images heal, but imperfectly.

We discover parts of ourselves which came to exist under this influential sign.

DEAD HAND

Temptations still nest in it like basilisks.
Hang it up till the rings fall.

ACCLIMATIZATION

I entered at the top of my voice. I forget the song.
It came over me that they were deaf. They gave me
Their praise and left me mute.

I proceeded among them
Like a tourist liner among coin-divers.
I flung them what I had with me. Only then
I saw that their smiles were made of gold, and their
Hands and their wives. They gave me
Their thanks and left me penniless.

It was my fault, I
Got hungry, they fed me. I gave them
My solemn word in payment. And all
The bells in the city rang in triumph
Like cash registers. They gave me their credit
And left me with little hope.
When I woke I discovered
That they had taken my legs leaving me the shoes.

(Oh priceless city, the buildings
Rising at dawn to grip the first light
Like bars, and the mornings shattered
With trees into all the shapes of heartbreak!)

I sit among them
Smiling, but they
Demand, they demand, they demand.

There is no putting them off.
Theirs is the empire, and beyond the empire
There is only ignorance, where I could not survive
Without feet.
To deceive them is to perish. What
Do I have that is my own? I offer my
Degradation as a blind beggar offers his palm.
And I am given
This glass eye to set in the place of tears.

THE SAINT OF THE UPLANDS

for Margot Pitt-Rivers

Their prayers still swarm on me like lost bees.
I have no sweetness. I am dust
Twice over.
       In the high barrens
The light loved us.
Their faces were hard crusts like their farms
And the eyes empty, where vision
Might not come otherwise
Than as water.

They were born to stones; I gave them
Nothing but what was theirs.
I taught them to gather the dew of their nights
Into mirrors. I hung them
Between heavens.

I took a single twig from the tree of my ignorance
And divined the living streams under
Their very houses. I showed them
The same tree growing in their dooryards.
You have ignorance of your own, I said.
They have ignorance of their own.

Over my feet they waste their few tears.

I taught them nothing.
Everywhere
The eyes are returning under the stones. And over
My dry bones they build their churches, like wells.

17

THE NAILS

I gave you sorrow to hang on your wall
Like a calendar in one color.
I wear a torn place on my sleeve.
It isn't as simple as that.

Between no place of mine and no place of yours
You'd have thought I'd know the way by now
Just from thinking it over.
Oh I know
I've no excuse to be stuck here turning
Like a mirror on a string,
Except it's hardly credible how
It all keeps changing.
Loss has a wider choice of directions
Than the other thing.

As if I had a system
I shuffle among the lies
Turning them over, if only
I could be sure what I'd lost.
I uncover my footprints, I
Poke them till the eyes open.
They don't recall what it looked like.
When was I using it last?
Was it like a ring or a light
Or the autumn pond
Which chokes and glitters but
Grows colder?

It could be all in the mind. Anyway
Nothing seems to bring it back to me.

And I've been to see
Your hands as trees borne away on a flood,
The same film over and over,
And an old one at that, shattering its account
To the last of the digits, and nothing
And the blank end.

The lightning has shown me the scars of the future.

I've had a long look at someone
Alone like a key in a lock
Without what it takes to turn.

It isn't as simple as that.

Winter will think back to your lit harvest
For which there is no help, and the seed
Of eloquence will open its wings
When you are gone.
But at this moment
When the nails are kissing the fingers good-bye
And my only
Chance is bleeding from me,
When my one chance is bleeding,
For speaking either truth or comfort
I have no more tongue than a wound.

SIRE

Here comes the shadow not looking where it is going,
And the whole night will fall; it is time.
Here comes the little wind which the hour
Drags with it everywhere like an empty wagon through leaves.
Here comes my ignorance shuffling after them
Asking them what they are doing.

Standing still, I can hear my footsteps
Come up behind me and go on
Ahead of me and come up behind me and
With different keys clinking in the pockets,
And still I do not move. Here comes
The white-haired thistle seed stumbling past through the branches
Like a paper lantern carried by a blind man.
I believe it is the lost wisdom of my grandfather
Whose ways were his own and who died before I could ask.

Forerunner, I would like to say, silent pilot,
Little dry death, future,
Your indirections are as strange to me
As my own. I know so little that anything
You might tell me would be a revelation.

Sir, I would like to say,
It is hard to think of the good woman
Presenting you with children, like cakes,
Granting you the eye of her needle,
Standing in doorways, flinging after you

20

Little endearments, like rocks, or her silence
Like a whole Sunday of bells. Instead, tell me:
Which of my many incomprehensions
Did you bequeath me, and where did they take you? Standing
In the shoes of indecision, I hear them
Come up behind me and go on ahead of me
Wearing boots, on crutches, barefoot, they could never
Get together on any door-sill or destination—
The one with the assortment of smiles, the one
Jailed in himself like a forest, the one who comes
Back at evening drunk with despair and turns
Into the wrong night as though he owned it—oh small
Deaf disappearance in the dusk, in which of their shoes
Will I find myself tomorrow?

FINALLY

My dread, my ignorance, my
Self, it is time. Your imminence
Prowls the palms of my hands like sweat.
Do not now, if I rise to welcome you,
Make off like roads into the deep night.
The dogs are dead at last, the locks toothless,
The habits out of reach.
I will not be false to you tonight.

Come, no longer unthinkable. Let us share
Understanding like a family name. Bring
Integrity as a gift, something
Which I had lost, which you found on the way.
I will lay it beside us, the old knife,
While we reach our conclusions.

Come. As a man who hears a sound at the gate
Opens the window and puts out the light
The better to see out into the dark,
Look, I put it out.

THE SHIPS ARE MADE READY IN SILENCE

Moored to the same ring:
The hour, the darkness and I,
Our compasses hooded like falcons.

Now the memory of you comes aching in
With a wash of broken bits which never left port,
In which once we planned voyages.
They come knocking like hearts asking:
What departures on this tide?

Breath of land, warm breath,
You tighten the cold around the navel,
Though all shores but the first have been foreign,
And the first was not home until left behind.

Our choice is ours but we have not made it,
Containing as it does, our destination
Circled with loss as with coral, and
A destination only until attained.

I have left you my hope to remember me by,
Though now there is little resemblance.
At this moment I could believe in no change,
The mast perpetually
Vacillating between the same constellations,
The night never withdrawing its dark virtue
From the harbor shaped as a heart,
The sea pulsing as a heart,

The sky vaulted as a heart,
Where I know the light will shatter like a cry
Above a discovery:
"Emptiness.
Emptiness! Look!"
Look. This is the morning.

ROUTE WITH NO NUMBER

If you want to come after me for any reason
I have left money in the bread-box,
Heart in the ice-box,
And in the mail-box, around the key,
A handkerchief for good-byes.

When you come to the end of the avenue of promises
And the dead bird falls from the limb
Turn away. It is the far fork. When you
Reach the street of the burying beetles
Follow their music as far as it will take you, skirting
The park where the famous
Sleep on their secrets.
And where the shout of the statue has filled
The square with long-dead silence,
Left.
At the turnstile of the hesitants I have left
A ticket for you in a little bee hole at eye level.
The toll keeper is not honest but he is
Cowardly and he has no legs.
Then in the empty boulevard with its view
Of the revolving hills you will see no car-tracks
But you will hear the sound of a street-car and discover
That the road is moving under your feet, it is
Not bad: rows of portraits on either side
Like cell windows along a corridor, and
Your shadow ducking its head as it passes.

Oh it's passable, and besides I contrive
As I always did, to keep thinking
Of improvements, for instance
The other day ducks went over on their creaking wings
So I thought, "In the future there will be
No more migration, only travel,
No more exile, only distances."
Also it's hard to convey how indifferent
I had become to the jabber of bells
And the senseless applause of clocks.
And then today, without warning, at a place
Where they speak no language, the collectors came through
For my back taxes my present taxes
And my future taxes whether I arrive or not.
I fooled them of course in the old way.
And they fooled me in the old way
And took everything but a few false decisions in the old way,
And I pray for them in the old way:
May the tracks be laid over them
And their fingers be picked off like daisy petals:
"She loathes me, she loathes me not."

Either way, I must tell you, in my present place
I can't hold out hope or any other flags.
There's not even a little privacy: you can see
Eyes lined up to ripen on all the sills.
And once here you're better than I am
If you can find your way back again.
However, I have visited the Day of the Dog,
But it was not yet open and I passed on.
Tell Mrs. H. just the same,
Who said I'd never get anywhere.

What a juncture.
I have gone faithfully into all the churches
And passed on, disappointed.
I have seen streets where the hands of the beggars
Are left out at night like shoes in a hotel corridor.
Several I thought had once been mine and might be again.
I have found many lost things and I have left them that way,
I have created enough disturbance.
I have come on many wasted things.
I have not yet come to my youth.

Now I am sitting
Behind filthy nightscapes, in the echoing room provided,
Among a few retired ornaments.
All the words have been emptied from the books.
The heating is hopeless at any hour. I am
Eating one of my last apples and waiting
For my departure to overtake me
With its empty windows coming up
Like cards, the game
Always turns out the same,
Mother, Father, Luke and John,
My line, my sign, my love,
Think of the cards that were held out to me
And I had to choose this one!

TO MY BROTHER HANSON

B. *Jan. 28, 1926*   D. *Jan. 28, 1926*

My elder,
Born into death like a message into a bottle,
The tide
Keeps coming in empty on the only shore.
Maybe it has lovers but it has few friends.
It is never still but it keeps its counsel, and

If I address you whose curious stars
Climbed to the tops of their houses and froze,
It is in hope of no
Answer, but as so often, merely
For want of another, for
I have seen catastrophe taking root in the mirror,
And why waste my words there?

Yes, now the roads themselves are shattered
As though they had fallen from a height, and the sky
Is cracked like varnish. Hard to believe,
Our family tree
Seems to be making its mark everywhere.
I carry my head high
On a pike that shall be nameless.

Even so, we had to give up honor entirely,
But I do what I can. I am patient
With the woes of the cupboards, and God knows—
I keep the good word close to hand like a ticket.
I feed the wounded lights in their cages.

28

I wake up at night on the penultimate stroke, and with
My eyes still shut I remember to turn the thorn
In the breast of the bird of darkness.
I listen to the painful song
Dropping away into sleep.

Blood
Is supposed to be thicker. You were supposed to be there
When the habits closed in pushing
Their smiles in front of them, when I was filled
With something else, like a thermometer,
When the moment of departure, standing
On one leg, like a sleeping stork, by the doorway,
Put down the other foot and opened its eye.
I
Got away this time for a while. I've come
Again to the whetted edge of myself where I
Can hear the hollow waves breaking like
Bottles in the dark. What about it? Listen, I've

Had enough of this. Is there nobody
Else in the family
To take care of the tree, to nurse the mirror,
To fix up a bite for hope when the old thing
Comes to the door,
To say to the pans of the balance
Rise up and walk?

IN THE NIGHT FIELDS

I heard the sparrows shouting "Eat, eat,"
And then the day dragged its carcass in back of the hill.
Slowly the tracks darkened.

The smoke rose steadily from no fires.
The old hunger, left in the old darkness,
Turned like a hanged knife.
I would have preferred a quiet life.
The bugs of regret began their services
Using my spine as a rosary. I left the maps
For the spiders.
Let's go, I said.

       Light of the heart,
The wheat had started lighting its lanterns,
And in every house in heaven there were lights waving
Hello good-bye. But that's
Another life.
Snug on the crumbling earth
The old bottles lay dreaming of new wine.
I picked up my breast, which had gone out.
By other lights I go looking for yours

Through the standing harvest of my lost arrows.
Under the moon the shadow
Practices mowing. Not for me, I say,
Please not for my
Benefit. A man cannot live by bread
Alone.

NOW AND AGAIN

Now that summer is lying with a stone for a lantern
You would think we could keep our thoughts
On the eyes of the living,

Those refugees,

Webs without spiders, needs without choice,
Lakes behind grids but without maps
Into which nothing keeps dropping like a stone.

Even our own.

Even the heart, that closed eye,
Has had its glimpses,
So that the marble lid winced and fluttered.

You would think we would know the present when it came,
And would remember what we knew,

And would recognize its fish-eyed children, able
To stare through tears forever
Not knowing them for sorrow and their own.

When you consider how learning happens
You would think once might be enough.
You would suppose such pain would become knowledge
And such knowledge would be wisdom
And such wisdom would stay with us.

Each time
The leaves hesitate but finally they fall.

The stars that came with us this far have gone back.
The wings of the migrants wake into autumn, and through
The hammered leaves the walnuts
Drop to the road and open:
Here is the small brain of our extinct summer.
Already it remembers nothing.

ANOTHER YEAR COME

I have nothing new to ask of you,
Future, heaven of the poor.
I am still wearing the same things.

I am still begging the same question
By the same light,
Eating the same stone,

And the hands of the clock still knock without entering.

OCTOBER

I remember how I would say, "I will gather
These pieces together,
Any minute now I will make
A knife out of a cloud."
Even then the days
Went leaving their wounds behind them,
But, "Monument," I kept saying to the grave,
"I am still your legend."

There was another time
When our hands met and the clocks struck
And we lived on the point of a needle, like angels.

I have seen the spider's triumph
In the palm of my hand. Above
My grave, that thoroughfare,
There are words now that can bring
My eyes to my feet, tamed.
Beyond the trees wearing names that are not their own
The paths are growing like smoke.

The promises have gone,
Gone, gone, and they were here just now.
There is the sky where they laid their fish.
Soon it will be evening.

DEPARTURE'S GIRL-FRIEND

Loneliness leapt in the mirrors, but all week
I kept them covered like cages. Then I thought
Of a better thing.

And though it was late night in the city
There I was on my way
To my boat, feeling good to be going, hugging
This big wreath with the words like real
Silver: *Bon Voyage.*

            The night
Was mine but everyone's, like a birthday.
Its fur touched my face in passing. I was going
Down to my boat, my boat,
To see if off, and glad at the thought.
Some leaves of the wreath were holding my hands
And the rest waved good-bye as I walked, as though
They were still alive.

And all went well till I came to the wharf, and no one.

I say no one, but I mean
There was this young man, maybe
Out of the merchant marine,
In some uniform, and I knew who he was; just the same
When he said to me where do you think you're going,
I was happy to tell him.

But he said to me, it isn't your boat,
You don't have one. I said, it's mine, I can prove it:
Look at this wreath I'm carrying to it,
Bon Voyage. He said, this is the stone wharf, lady,
You don't own anything here.
                                        And as I
Was turning away, the injustice of it
Lit up the buildings, and there I was
In the other and hated city
Where I was born, where nothing is moored, where
The lights crawl over the stone like flies, spelling now,
Now, and the same fate chances roll
Their many eyes; and I step once more
Through a hoop of tears and walk on, holding this
Buoy of flowers in front of my beauty,
Wishing myself the good voyage.

ONE WAY

Oh hell, there once again hunger
Gets up in the middle of a meal and without
A word departs. I go after: what
Would I be without her?

                       It is
Night, I am
As old as pain and I have
No other story.
We do not keep to the telegraph lines.
"Is there a map for this?" I call
After. "Is there even
A name for this? I spend my
Life asking, is there even a name
For you?"

          And what a starved path,
Licking stones; often
I am sure one side has eaten the other.
And with what bitterness I remember
I had not yet had my fill
Of dissatisfaction. My mouth
Works like a heart. More and more
I get like shadows; I find out
How they hate.
               And then she is gone.

No astonishment anywhere. The owls

Are digesting in silence.
I will not look up again to learn again
That despair has no star.
Don't ask me why, I
Lift my feet in their dice-boxes.
I believe I continue
As she would have done, I believe.

                                       Don't ask me
Why: this time it is not I
Waking the birds. Somewhere
The light begins to come to itself.
As I walk, the horizon
Climbs down from its tree and moves toward me
With offerings. There
At the table which she has set with
The old plates, she is waiting, and to us
The day returns like a friend
Bringing others.

RECOGNITION

The bird of ash has appeared at windows
And the roads will turn away, mourning.
What distances we survived, the fire
With its one wing
And I with my blackened heart.

I came home as a web to its spider,
To teach the flies of my household
Their songs. I walked
In on the mirrors scarred as match-boxes,
The gaze of the frames and the ticking
In the beams. The shadows
Had grown a lot and they clung
To the skirts of the lamps.
Nothing
Remembered who I was.

The dead turn in their locks and
I wake like a hand on a handle. Tomorrow
Marches on the old walls, and there
Is my coat full of darkness in its place
On the door.
Welcome home,
Memory.

INVOCATION

The day hanging by its feet with a hole
In its voice
And the light running into the sand

Here I am once again with my dry mouth
At the fountain of thistles
Preparing to sing.

THE POEM

Coming late, as always,
I try to remember what I almost heard.
The light avoids my eye.

How many times have I heard the locks close
And the lark take the keys
And hang them in heaven.

SECOND SIGHT

Turning the corner I
Realize that I have read this before.
It is summer. The sun
Sits on the fire-escape while its children
Tear their voices into little shreds.
I wish I could remember how it ended.

This is the passage where the mirrors
Are embarking at the ends of the streets.
The drawn shades are waving
From empty rooms, and the old days
Are fanning themselves here and there on the steps.
The fact is, I have come back
Again and again, as a wish on a post-card, only
This time the jewels are turning
In the faces, and it seems I should know
The motive for the laundry, and the name
Of the man with the teeth, at intervals saying
You want to buy your time.

I feel this is a bit that I know how it goes;
I should be able to call
Most of the windows
By their christian names, they have whole
Chapters to themselves
Before the pigeons give up, and the brightest
Are reflections of darkness. But no,
They've got it wrong, they've got it wrong,

Like anywhere else.

It's the old story,
Every morning something different is real.
This place is no more than the nephew of itself,
With these cats, this traffic, these
Departures
To which I have kept returning,
Having tasted the apple of my eye,
Saying perennially
Here it is, the one and only,
The beginning and the end.
This time the dials have come with the hands and
Suddenly I was never here before.
Oh dust, oh dust, progress
Is being made.

Evening has brought its
Mouse and let it out on the floor,
On the wall, on the curtain, on
The clock. You with the gloves, in the doorway,
Who asked you to come and watch?

As the bats flower in the crevices
You and your brothers
Raise your knives to see by.
Surely the moon can find her way to the wells
Without you. And the streams
To their altars.

As for us, we enter your country
With our eyes closed.

THE INDIGESTION OF THE VAMPIRE

Look at this red pear
Hanging from a good family

Where the butcher hung the rag on the tree.

The bat's bloated again,
Hooked on his dark nimbus
Getting over it.
Here is the cure of pity
Upside down.

Elsewhere the laundry
Is buried,
The deer tracks left by his teeth
Look for the cross-roads,
The veins that are still good
Hold out their hands.

Here's his story.

His bridges are not burned only folded.
In a while the swollen life
He calls his own
Will shrink back till it fits the mirrors,
No worse for no wear;
The eyes will come
To conceal movement again;

He will find his voice to fly by.

That's how he does it: rock-a-bye,
Hanging there with his silence all wool
And others at heart,
Two pounds in his pound bag,

Shaped like a tear but
Not falling for anyone.

THE SINGER

The song dripping from the eaves,
I know that throat

With no tongue,
Ignoring sun and moon,

That glance, that creature
Returning to its heart

By whose light the streams
Find each other.

Untameable,
Incorruptible,

In its own country
It has a gate to guard.

There arrived without choice
Take up water

And lay it on your eyes saying
Hail clarity

From now on nothing
Will appear the same

And pass through
Leaving your salt behind.

THE CONTINUO

What can you do with this
Wind, you can't
Reason with it, entertain it, send
It back, live on it or with it, fold it
Away and forget it, coming at you

All the time perfectly
Empty no face no background,
Before you know it, needing
No doors,
Lighting out of trees, flags, windows of
Fallen buildings, with a noise that could
Run its own trains, what
Can you learn from it

Leaving its shoes all over the place
Turning day and night into
Back yards
Where it knows the way.

VOCATIONS

I
Simplicity, if you
Have any time
Where do you spend it?
I tempt you with clear water.
All day I hang out a blue eye. All night
I long for the sound of your small bell
Of an unknown metal.

II
Seeing how it goes
I see how it will be:
The color leaves but the light stays,
The light stays but we cannot grasp it,
We leave the tree rocking its
Head in its hands and we
Go indoors.

III
The locked doors of the night were still sitting in their circle.
I recalled the promises of the bridges.
I got up and made my way
To wash my shadow in the river.
In a direction that was lost
The hands of the water have found tomorrow.

AIR

Naturally it is night.
Under the overturned lute with its
One string I am going my way
Which has a strange sound.

This way the dust, that way the dust.
I listen to both sides
But I keep right on.
I remember the leaves sitting in judgment
And then winter.

I remember the rain with its bundle of roads.
The rain taking all its roads.
Nowhere.

Young as I am, old as I am,

I forget tomorrow, the blind man.
I forget the life among the buried windows.
The eyes in the curtains.
The wall
Growing through the immortelles.
I forget silence
The owner of the smile.

This must be what I wanted to be doing,
Walking at night between the two deserts,
Singing.

THE PRESENT

The walls join hands and
It is tomorrow:
The birds clucking to the horses, the horses
Doing the numbers for the hell of it,
The numbers playing the calendars,
The saints marching in,
It seems only yesterday,
                            when what
I keep saying to myself is
Take a leaf from the fire, open
Your hand, see
Where you are going,
When what I am trying to find is
The beginning,
In the ashes,
A wing, when what we are looking for
In each other
Is each other,

The stars at noon,

While the light worships its blind god.

STANDARDS

Nothing will do but
I must get a new flag,
I've buried enough under this one,

And then there are my
Followers, mad for a bit of color,
Damn them,

And the end I suppose is not yet,
The way the trees come beating
Their horses, and the wheat is camped
Under its dead crow,
The rivers under themselves. And I'm not ready
To just sit down and let the horizon
Ride over me.

Maybe I thought
I could go on and on flying the same rag,
Like the fire,
But it's faded white and I'm
Not the fire, I'll have to find
Something bright and simple to signify
Me, what an order.

What an order but I'll have to do something.
Up until now the pulse
Of a stone was my flag
And the stone's in pieces.

FROM A SERIES

Division, mother of pain,
Look at you bringing
Your children up just as formerly
And look at me back again
In this former life,
You've all grown but I haven't.

You might as well ask me why
I come back to a month
Alright
Why do I and when I think
There used to be eleven others
At one time as they say and those
Other days in the week
I see the posters have changed
But the day's the same and even
When it was here hope would wait
Out in the garden rocking the grave
Now she's dead too and that's a blessing.

Just the same it was nice the way
You had them trained
And as for me it was nice
The way I used to be able
To forget between
The last time I learned and the next time;
The way I loved
The east and the west my horses;

It had its points, surely, if only
I could have been one at a time.
How long

Can the hands of the clock go on drowning
Without my helping
One way or the other
How long
Before freedom looms in front of me
And the door falls in on my tongue?

BREAD AND BUTTER

I keep finding this letter
To the gods of abandon,
Tearing it up: Sirs,
Having lived in your shrines
I know what I owe you—

I don't, did I ever? With both hands
I've forgotten, I keep
Having forgotten. I'll have no such shrines here.
I will not bow in the middle of the room
To the statue of nothing
With the flies turning around it.
On these four walls I am the writing.

Why would I start such a letter?
Think of today, think of tomorrow.
Today on the tip of my tongue,
Today with my eyes,
Tomorrow the vision,
Tomorrow

In the broken window
The broken boats will come in,
The life boats
Waving their severed hands,

And I will love as I ought to
Since the beginning.

WE CONTINUE

For Galway Kinnell

The rust, a little pile of western color, lies
At the end of its travels,
Our instrument no longer.

Those who believe
In death have their worship cut out for them.
As for myself, we
Continue,

An old
Scar of light our trumpet,

Pilgrims with thorns
To the eye of the cold
Under flags made by the blind,
In one fist

This letter that vanishes
If the hand opens:

Charity, come home,
Begin.

MARICA LART

Now
We do not even know
What to wish for you

Oh sleep rocked
In an empty hand.

REUNION

At the foot of your dry well,
Old friend in ambush,
What did we expect?

Have we really changed?
You could never forgive me for
Pleasures divulged or defeats kept secret.

You have flowered in your little heat
Like an untrimmed wick.
It is plain what you are thinking

While I am thinking
How you have grown into your ugliness
Which at one time did not fit you.

Console your distaste for departures:
I find I brought only the one.
Hand me my coat.

Friend Reductio,
Would you have known delight
If it had knocked you down?

WALK-UP

The inspector of stairs is on the stairs
Oh my God and I thought it was Sunday,
His advance like a broom and those stairs going
Down to meet him, alright
What that's mine will he show me
To be ashamed of this time

The spiders in my face, the whistles
In the cupboards,
The darkness in my shoes, going out
To deep water

        No

The sky's at home in these windows, and the maps
Of themselves on these walls,
And your letter is enough improvement
For anywhere, lying open
On my table, my
Love

      I won't close a thing

Let him arrive fanning himself
With his calendar, let him become
At the door the inspector of doors and find
Mine open,
Inspector of hands—

His name
Would mean nothing to me, his questions are not
His own, but let my answers
Be mine.

TO WHERE WE ARE

With open arms the water runs in to the wheel.

I come back to where I have never been.
You arrive to join me.
We have the date in our hands.

We come on to where we are, laughing to think
Of the Simplicities in their shapeless hats
With a door so they can sit outside it

I hope I may say
Our neighbors

Natives of now, creatures of
One song,
Their first, their last,

Listen.

THE CROSSROADS OF THE WORLD ETC.

I would never have thought I would be born here

So late in the stone so long before morning
Between the rivers learning of salt

Memory my city

Hope my city Ignorance my city
With my teeth on your chessboard black and white
What is your name

With my dead on your
Calendar with my eyes
In your paint
Opening
With my grief on your bridges with my voice
In your stones what is your name
Typed in rain while I slept

The books just give
The names of locks
The old books names of old locks
Some have stopped beating

Photos of
Dead doors left to right still hide
The beginning
Which do you

Open if
Any
My shadow crosses them trying to strike a light

Today is in another street

I'm coming to that
Before me

The bird of the end with its
Colorless feet
Has walked on windows

I lose the track but I find it
Again again
Memory

In the mirrors the star called Nothing

Cuts us off

Wait for me

Ruin
My city
Oh wreck of the future out of which
The future rises
What is your name as we fall

As the mortar
Falls between the faces
As the one-legged man watching the chess game

Falls
As the moon withers in the blueprint
And from our graves these curtains blow

These clouds on which I have written
Hope

As I
Have done
Hearing the light flowing over a knife
And autumn on the posters

Hearing a shadow beating a bell
Ice cream in ambulances, a chain full of fingers
The trains on the
Trestles faster than their lights
The new scars around the bend
Arriving

Hearing the day pass talking to itself
Again
Another life

Once a key in another country
Now ignorance
Ignorance

I keep to your streets until they vanish
There is singing beyond
The addresses can I
Let it go home alone

A playing on veins a lark in a lantern

It conducts me to a raw Sabbath

On all sides bread
Has been begged, here are monuments
At their feet this
Section
The tubes tied off the cry gone

The cry
I would never have thought
The lightning rises and sets

Rust, my brothers, stone, my brothers,
Hung your spirits on the high hooks
Can't reach them now

You've swallowed night I swallow night
I will swallow night
And lie among the games of papers
And the gills of nibbling
Fires

Will I

While the sky waits in the station like a man
With no place to go

Will I

I hear my feet in a tunnel but I move

Like a tear on a doorsill
It's now in my wrist

Ahead of me under
False teeth hanging from a cloud, his
Sign that digs for his house, Tomorrow,
The oldest man
Is throwing food into empty cages

Is it to me
He turns his cobweb
I go toward him extending
My shadow taking it to him
Is it to me he says no

Is it to me
He says no no I haven't time

Keep the lost garment, where would I find the owner?

RESOLUTION

Back of the door the child is playing that
Piano drawn on a piece of paper
He keeps to the black notes it
Gets dark
He moves to the white notes it gets
Too dark I can't hear him any more

As I was

The customs men multiply between
He takes with him
Memory leaking feathers
If he knew what I
Know now in the same X-ray

The pictures turn to the walls here is
Death the same taste in
A different color
Thinks I will say it

The scars
Grow leaves the feeling
Runs ahead and hides in bushes with its
Knives painted out
I know

Thinks I will say
It say it

As the hole climbs the sky

Oh let it be yesterday surely
It's time

Never

Never

A usage I'm learning a beak at my ear
I hear

The hearts in bottles
The dice lying awake

The clock dropping its shoes and
No floor.

BEFORE THAT

It was never there and already it's vanishing

City unhealthy pale with pictures of
    Cemeteries sifting on its windows
    Its planets with wind in their eyes searching among
    The crosses again
    At night
    In dark clothes

    It was never there

    Papers news from the desert
    Moving on or
    Lying in cages
    Wrapping for their
    Voices

    The river flowing past its other shore
    Past the No Names the windows washed at night
    And who is my
    Name for

    In my pocket
    Slowly the photographs becoming saints
    Never there

    I put out my hand and the dark falls through it
    Following a flag

Gutters made in my time rounded with
The wounded in mind
The streets roped off for the affectionate
Will do for the
Mutilated

If I
Lie down in the street and that smoke comes out of me

Who
Was it

It was a night like this that the ashes were made

Before that
Was always the fire

FOR THE GRAVE OF POSTERITY

This stone that is
not here and bears no writing commemorates
the emptiness at the end of
history listen you without vision you can still
hear it there is
nothing it is the voice with the praises
that never changed that called to the unsatisfied
as long as there was
time
whatever it could have said of you is already forgotten

THIS DAY OF THIS MONTH OF THIS YEAR
OF THIS

How can I persuade today that it's
                    Here how can I
Say   My
        Love

        Outlined in knives

        I'm tracing you with an
        Opened finger the eye
        Of my thumb is awake
                            Is not
        This your home where are you
        Is not this
        Your home

        Drunks on the compass feathers on the floor yes here

        Where the river flows around our suitcases
        Where the light shakes the buildings
        Where they teach silence in both schools on this block but
        The streets give
                            Cry give cry all the time

        Where Easter the phantom hounds the Holy Rollers
        Where the months are shot at midnight by
        A cop in civvies in a dark car on a side street

        Where my birth came upon me comes upon me where

My hand that found the hand
Of day finds the hand of
Absence

Where my arm is smoke

Before the two cripples pass on their one crutch
Before the spittle rises from the sidewalk
Before the darkness comes out of the
Trumpet
Tunnel to itself subway with
No platform

                         I want
To declare myself

I want to declare Now

Her name is now wherever she is
      There is none beside her

           For whom my hands were split
I want
To make time with her under the same flag
Running water with running water I want
To point out the sights ahead of us would
There be sights ahead of us

With my story

With the child I left to die
           Dying

With the love I wrapped in a map
                    There
With the uniform I wore
                    Black
                    As they all are

With my teeth graveyard for the nameless
With extinction my ancestor
With a fresh sparrow caught in the headlines
With the funerals in the bridges
                    From which the music
                    With
My lungs full of ashes
With what I empty from my shoes

With the other calendar other
        Facade in which I have a darkness
        Marked X to which my key marked X

        X in my hand in both hands
        X waiting

Oh with
        Death testing itself in my ocean cream in my coffee
        Death my window at which the birds come to drink at night

Oh with your face her face your
Face invisible

With death my hands

With my hands nothing oh with death my words

74

With my words nothing
One at a time

Oh with death my
Heart
With my heart

Lantern of ice

Oh with her shoes
                Hanging
                In the clock

THE WAY TO THE RIVER

for Dido

The way to the river leads past the names of
Ash the sleeves the wreaths of hinges
Through the song of the bandage vendor

I lay your name by my voice
As I go

The way to the river leads past the late
Doors and the games of the children born looking backwards
They play that they are broken glass
The numbers wait in the halls and the clouds
Call
From windows
They play that they are old they are putting the horizon
Into baskets they are escaping they are
Hiding

I step over the sleepers the fires the calendars
My voice turns to you

I go past the juggler's condemned building the hollow
Windows gallery
Of invisible presidents the same motion in them all
In a parked cab by the sealed wall the hats are playing
Sort of poker with somebody's
Old snapshots game I don't understand they lose
The rivers one
After the other I begin to know where I am

I am home

Be here the flies from the house of the mapmaker
Walk on our letters I can tell
And the days hang medals between us
I have lit our room with a glove of yours be
Here I turn
To your name and the hour remembers
Its one word
Now

Be here what can we
Do for the dead the footsteps full of money
I offer you what I have my
Poverty

To the city of wires I have brought home a handful
Of water I walk slowly
In front of me they are building the empty
Ages I see them reflected not for long
Be here I am no longer ashamed of time it is too brief its hands
Have no names
I have passed it I know

    Oh Necessity you with the face you with
    All the faces

This is written on the back of everything

But we
Will read it together

SHE WHO WAS GONE

Passage of lights without hands
Passage of hands without lights
This water between

I take in my arms

My love whose names I cannot say
Not knowing them and having a tongue
Of dust

My love with light flowing on her like tears

She on whom the bruise went sailing
She who was a shoe on a pillow
She who was gone

Under empty socks hanging mouth downward from the bridges
Under the color of no one
While feathers went on falling in the doorways

She who with a blank ticket waited
Under a flag made of flies while the sun brought
Blood in eyecups

I take in my arms

My love from the valley of dice my love in the valley of dice
Among the flowers smelling of lightning

My love on whom the light has forgotten nothing

We say good-bye distance we are here
We can say it quietly who else is there
We can say it with silence our native tongue

MY FRIENDS

My friends without shields walk on the target

It is late the windows are breaking

My friends without shoes leave
What they love
Grief moves among them as a fire among
Its bells
My friends without clocks turn
On the dial they turn
They part

My friends with names like gloves set out
Bare handed as they have lived
And nobody knows them
It is they that lay the wreaths at the milestones it is their
Cups that are found at the wells
And are then chained up

My friends without feet sit by the wall
Nodding to the lame orchestra
Brotherhood it says on the decorations
My friend without eyes sits in the rain smiling
With a nest of salt in his hand

My friends without fathers or houses hear
Doors opening in the darkness
Whose halls announce

Behold the smoke has come home

My friends and I have in common
The present a wax bell in a wax belfry
This message telling of
Metals this
Hunger for the sake of hunger this owl in the heart
And these hands one
For asking one for applause

My friends with nothing leave it behind
In a box
My friends without keys go out from the jails it is night
They take the same road they miss
Each other they invent the same banner in the dark
They ask their way only of sentries too proud to breathe

At dawn the stars on their flag will vanish

The water will turn up their footprints and the day will rise
Like a monument to my
Friends the forgotten

THE MAN WHO WRITES ANTS

Their eggs named for his eyes I suppose
Their eggs his tears
His memory
                    Into
The ground into the walls over the sills

At each cross road
He has gone

With his days he has gone ahead
            Called by what trumpet

His words on the signs
His tears at their feet
            Growing wings

I know him from tunnels by side roads
I know him

Not his face if he has one

I know him by his writings I am
Tempted to draw him
As I see him
Sandals stride flag on his shoulder ship on it signalling
Mask on the back of his head
Blind

Called

By what trumpet

He leaves my eyes he climbs my graves
I pass the names

He is not followed I am not following him no

Today the day of the water
With ink for my remote purpose with my pockets full of black
With no one in sight
I am walking in silence I am walking in silence I am walking
In single file listening for a trumpet

THE NEXT

The funeral procession swinging empty belts
Walks on the road on the black rain
Though the one who is dead was not ready

In the casket lid the nails are still turning

Behind it come the bearers
Of tires and wet pillows and the charred ladder
And the unrollers of torn music and a picture of smoke
And last the boy trailing the long
String cut off clean
Whom a voice follows calling Why a white one
When a red one would have done just as well

Under the casket the number
Is scratched out with signs of haste

We let it go we gather with other persuaders
In the parlor of the house of The Next
And I in my wax shoes my mind goes back
To the last dead Who was it I say

Could it have been my friend the old man
With the wet dog and the shed where he
Slept on a ladder till the whole place burned
Here just now was his other
Friend the carpenter
Who was besides a crusher of shells for cement

No they say he was months ago this was no one we knew
But he was one of us

We let it go we are
Gathered with other persuaders in the parlor
The Next is upstairs he is
Ten feet tall hale and solid his bed is no deathbed
He is surrounded by friends they enjoy the secret of safety
They are flush they are candle-lit they move to laughter
Downstairs it is not yet known
Who will go instead of him this time
Like the others one after the other because they were scared

The laughter keeps time on the stairs

These words start rising out of my wax shoes I
Say we must tell him
We must go up there we must go up there and You
Are The Next we must tell him
The persuaders say he would deafen us
When we say No no one hears us

My shoes are softening but at the same time I am saying
Someone would help us and it would be us
Even the carpenter would
Help us when he went out he said
He would not be gone long
Removing a knocker from a door
And the caskets are clearly numbered not ours we
Must rise under the turning nails
I say to the persuaders downstairs in the house of The Next

And when they say Yes no one hears them

THE STUDENTS OF JUSTICE

All night I hear the hammers
Of the blind men in the next building
Repairing their broken doors

When it is silent it is
That they are gone
Before the sun lights the way for
The young thieves

All day the blind neighbors are at their lesson
Coloring a rough book
Oh a long story
And under their white hair they keep forgetting

It tells of gorges hung with high caves and
Little rotting flags
And through the passes caravans of bugs
Bearing away our blood in pieces

What can be done what can be done

They take their hammers to the lesson

The last words so they promise me
Will be thank you and they will know why

And that night they will be allowed to move

Every day
They leave me their keys which they never use

AN ISLAND IN THE HARBOR

My own country my countrymen the exchanges
Yes this is the place

The flag of the blank wall the birds of money

Prisoners in the watch towers
And the motto
>   *The hopes of others our*
>   *Guardians*

Even here
Spring passes looking for the cradles

The beating on the bars of the cages
Is caught and parcelled out to the bells

It is twelve the prisoners' own hour

The mouse bones in the plaster
Prepare for the resurrection

MOUNTAIN TOWN

My memory the invisible buffalo
Lumbers through the vacant street
Considering the fences their

Sorrows

And the lightning died in its
Mine oh it must be
Some time back its name
Is written everywhere in faded
Dust

One of its
Gloves wheels on the sky over
The blind movie
And the station where the white train still
Attends

A bell that I hung onto as long as I could
Is about to arrive and start ringing

FOR NOW

The year a bird flies against the drum

I come to myself miles away with
Tickets dying in my hand

You are not here will the earth last till you come
I must say now what cannot
Be said later Goodbye
The name of the statues but who needs them
As for myself I

Look back at the rain
I grew up in the rooms of the rain
So that was home so let the grass grow
Goodbye faces in stains churches
In echoes dusters at windows
Schools without floors envelopes full of smoke
Goodbye hands of those days I keep the fossils
Goodbye iron Bible containing my name in rust
Cock Robin and
The date
Goodbye Cock Robin I never saw you

On plates upside down in token of mourning
I eat to your vanishing

I bearing messages

With all my words my silence being one

From childhood to childhood the
Message Goodbye from the shoulders of victory
To the followers
From the sea to the nearest of kin

From the roller skates to the death in the basement
From the lightning to
Its nest from myself to my name
Goodbye

I begin with what was always gone

Ancestors in graves of broken glass
In empty cameras

Mistakes in the mail Goodbye to the same name

Goodbye what you learned for me I have to learn anyway

You that forgot your rivers they are gone
Myself I would not know you

Goodbye as
The eyes of a whale say goodbye having never seen
Each other

And to you that vanished as I watched goodbye
Walter the First
Jacques the Clown
Marica the Good

Goodbye pain of the past that
Will never be made better goodbye
Pain of the innocent that will never
Not have existed
Goodbye you that are
Buried with the name of the florist in your hands
And a box from our
Box society your finger holding the place
Your jaws tied with a ribbon marked Justice
To help us

The dead say Look
The living in their distress sink upward weeping
But who could reach them in such a sea

Goodbye kites painted with open mouths over the
Scarlet road of the animals

Goodbye prophets sometimes we are
Here sometimes we remember it
Sometimes we walk in your
Eyes which sometimes you lost
Sometimes we walk in your old brains and are forgotten

Or this character gets on the bus with an open razor
Bends down to my face at once thinking he
Knows me goodbye
Yard where I was supposed
To be safe behind the fences of sand
Watched over by an empty parasol and the sound of
Pulleys I who
Had built the ark

Goodbye cement street address of cement tears
Grief of the wallpaper the witness
Cold banisters worn thin with fright
Photo of me wondering what it would be like
The girls at last the hips full of dice the names
In smoke for the lamps the
Calling Goodbye among the wishes
Among the horses

If I had known what to say there would be the same hands
Holding white crosses in front of the windows

Goodbye to the dew my master

And you masters with feathers on your key rings
Wardens of empty scales
When I find where I am goodbye

Goodbye sound of a voice spelling its name to a uniform
Spelling it
Again goodbye white
Truck that backs up to drugstores after dark
Arriving at
Apartment houses in the afternoon
And the neighbors calling can you come up for a minute

Goodbye anniversaries I pass without knowing
Days for which the chairs are wired
The law on the throne of ice above the salting floor
Its eyes full of falling snow
Friend Instead and the rest of the
Brothers Meaningless

Those who will drown next bow to their straws

Goodbye to the water a happy person
The longer its story the
Less it tells
Goodbye to the numbers starting with God

To the avenues
No one asked their permission so they had none

Goodbye hands wrapped in newspaper

And when the towers are finished the frameworks are
Thrown from the tops and descend slowly
Waving as they
Dissolve

Tell me what you see vanishing and I
Will tell you who you are
To whom I say Goodbye
You my neighbors in the windows in the registers you
The sizes of your clothes
You born with the faces of presidents on your eyelids

Tell me how your hands fall and I will tell you
What you will wave to next
Guests of yourselves expecting hosts
You in the cold of whose
Voices I can hear
The hanged man in the chimney turning
You with mouths full of pebbles
In the rising elevator in the falling building you

With your destinations written in your shoelaces
And your lies elected

They return in the same
Skins to the same seats by the flags of money
Goodbye to the Bibles hollowed for swearing on
A hole knocks on the panes but is not heard

Around them the crashes occur in silence
The darkness that flows from the sirens passes the windows
The blackness spreads from the headlines
Over their spectacles they light the ceilings

Goodbye what we may never see
Age would have kissed false teeth if any
Its caresses making a bed slowly
Even as a child I hoped it would spare me
I made tears for it I sang

As the cards are laid out they turn to ashes
I kiss
The light to those who love it it is brief

Goodbye before it is taken away
I have been with it the season could sign for me

The message sang in its bottle it would find me
I knew the king of the moths I knew the watchman's country
I knew where the phoebe lost herself I knew the story
I stepped in the lock I
Turned
My thumb was carved with the one map of a lost mountain

94

My scars will answer to no one but me
I know the planet that lights up the rings in the hems
I know the stars in the door

I know the martyrs sleeping in almonds
I know the gloves of the hours I know Pilate the fly
I know the enemy's brother

But it will happen just the same goodbye

Heart my elder

My habits of sand
My bones whose count is lost every night every day
The milestones of salt the rain my feet
Memory in its rivers
Goodbye my house my cat my spiders

Goodbye distance from whom I
Borrow my eyes goodbye my voice
In the monument of strangers goodbye to the sun
Among the wings nailed to the windows goodbye
My love

You that return to me through the mountain of flags
With my raven on your wrist
You with the same breath

Between death's republic and his kingdom

SPRING

On the water the first wind
Breaks it all up into arrows

The dead bowmen buried these many years

Are setting out again

And I
I take down from the door
My story with the holes
For the arms the face and the vitals
I take down the sights from the mantle
I'm going to my uncle the honest one
Who stole me the horse in the good cause

There's light in my shoes
I carry my bones on a drum
I'm going to my uncle the dog
The croupier the old horror
The one who takes me as I am

Like the rest of the devils he was born in heaven

Oh withered rain

Tears of the candles veins full of feathers
Knees in salt
I the bell's only son

Having spent one day in his house
Will have your answer

96

DAYBREAK

Again this procession of the speechless
Bringing me their words
The future woke me with its silence
I join the procession
An open doorway
Speaks for me
Again

W. S. MERWIN

W. S. Merwin was born in New York City in 1927 and grew up in Union City, New Jersey, and in Scranton, Pennsylvania. Besides poetry he has written articles, chiefly for *The Nation*, and radio scripts for the BBC.

From 1949 to 1951 he worked as a tutor in France, Portugal and Majorca. Since then he has made the greater part of his living by translating from French, Spanish, Latin and Portuguese. He has lived in England, France and the United States.

Mr. Merwin's previous books of poetry are *A Mask for Janus*, 1952, *The Dancing Bears*, 1954, *Green with Beasts*, 1956, and *The Drunk in the Furnace*, 1960. His translations include *The Poem of the Cid*, 1959, *Spanish Ballads*, 1960, *The Satires of Persius*, 1960, *Lazarillo de Tormes*, 1962, and *The Song of Roland*, 1963.